Wising Up, Dressing Down

Wising Up, Dressing Down

EDWARD MACKINNON

Shoestring Press

Typeset and Printed by Q3 Print Project Management Ltd, Loughborough (01509 213456)

Published by Shoestring Press
19 Devonshire Avenue, Beeston, Nottingham, NG9 1BS
Telephone: (0115) 925 1827
www.shoestringpress.co.uk

First published 2002
© Copyright: Edward Mackinnon
ISBN: 1 899549 66 8

Shoestring Press gratefully acknowledges financial assistance from East Midlands Arts

For Karin – ein Glück,
dass es Dich gibt

Acknowledgements

Acknowledgements are due to the editors of the following publications in which a number of these poems, or versions of these poems, first appeared: *Orbis, London Magazine, The Forward Book of Poetry 1995, Envoi, Iota, Scratch, The Dark Horse, Oasis, Cencrastus, The Rialto, Stand, The Penniless Press*, and *Staple*.

I would also like to record my special thanks to the late Alan Ross, Mike Shields and John Lucas for their kind encouragement and advice.

Contents

Hope balanced with despair. Imagination
intemperate. By the too well-contented
left cold. To keep warm,
rolling over the floor laughing.
And how to retain one's dignity?
By saying no. Walking
only the thinnest of lines.
Thus moving forward, against
the flow. CONTRARI-
WISE.

THE WHISKY TRAIL

You start with the tiniest of drams, to wind
yourself down for pleasant dreams, and when,
after months of manfully screwing up the eyes,
grimacing and spluttering, you realise
it's actually supposed to torture you
in this way, you join a club for connoisseurs,
acquire a nosing glass, ask for cask-strength
single malts and read expert appraisals
(e.g. smells "faintly musty but classy,
like an aristocratic fart"), and before long
you're planning to spend the summer holidays
on the Whisky Trail
                which leads straight back
to your father: who when he had over-imbibed
didn't see the world through the glass as you do
— translucent, redeemed, everyone absolving
one another — but turned aggressive, clattered
through the house like a bull with a branded head
and stomped off to bed muttering dark curses
against the English — who, it must be said, have
a lot to answer for, for instance:
                     James Stewart
of Acharn, called James of the Glen, scapegoated
in the days when the Highlands were subjugated
after Culloden, hanged and his corpse gibbeted
and its removal by his loved ones prevented
by guards, and this for years, till it was whittled
by crows and the bones bleached by wind and sun,
bones swung, bones dropped, bones were re-hung
as a warning to any bare-arsed caterans
of a mind to challenge the claret-drinking
civilisation that flowed north from London.

Blame the digression on the drink. But one thing
leads to another. And in the end you find
that everything comes back to bloody politics.
There's just no getting away from it. Not even
in the amber fluid that starts you raving
or makes you a maudlin fool. It's a shame.
I mean, it can destroy the grace of living.

ALMOST LIKE JOE MEEK'S BLUES

It was in those days after Holly and the music died, when pop
was in a slump. He contrived to get songs that were crap to the top
of the charts. His name was in *Melody Maker* nearly every week
and it seemed to me in my grammar school days as though Joe Meek
produced every other hit. I pictured him raking in the lolly,
a sharp lad on the make, living it up in London, with a dolly
bird on each arm. But like fluff blown off a stylus he disappeared
without a trace. In any case, the music business was now geared
to a new sound: the Beatles and the Stones. Pop started to boom again.
I was going up to Cambridge. The swinging sixties could now begin.

He blew his brains out while I was there. But at the time I never read
the half-column on the inside page. I found out long after he was dead
that Joe was no flash Harry, but a slightly gauche and moody queer
who had been twiddling knobs since boyhood, an ace recording
    engineer
who spoke in soft Cambridgeshire tones and lived in a modest pad
in Holloway where he built his studio. People thought him half-mad
as he trailed microphone cables to the bathroom, but this was the
    ground
on which he waged his private battle, creating his own distinctive sound
and taking on Tin Pan Alley. He won and lost. They were unforgiving.
Working with show biz pseuds must have been even worse than living

in Cambridge, where as a pimply youth in incongruous black gown
I played at being an undergrad, and the grey streets of the town
brooded like the Bergman films I went to see, and girls were rare.
But he was more of a misfit than me, for he had no-one to share
and sustain that dream from which all pop music starts. I had the luck
to have friends who helped me survive the Cambridge blues, and so I
    stuck
it out and got my degree. All he had was a lonely pride
in what he had achieved. In the end there was nowhere to hide
after being found guilty of importuning. He died of shame.
Poor Joe was queer, not gay. The swinging sixties never came.

ST KILDA

The better worlds too are not without blemishes.
Ill winds blew from all directions, the worst of them
a consequence of their diet of fat bird flesh.
But they let one wind contend with another
and let neither detract in the least from the pleasure
of al fresco democracy, the euphonious
sound of almost endless debate that was an end
in itself, the spiritual counterpoint to the need
to find food and such animal pleasures as ensued,
rest and respite from the giddy heights of the cliffs and stacks.

Nature defined them and they found it natural
to hold in common the means to life: the land
and what it bore and what was borne on the air:
feathers and flesh, eggs and oil and entrails of birds.
Nothing was wasted. For all was won together,
in a balancing act, just as brides were won
by suitors perched on a heel high above sea
on a stone, fitness for life and the wedded state
being one and embodied in thickened ankles
and prehensile toes that were the hold on their very existence.

Gannets, puffins, fulmars. Feathering their beds,
keeping lamps lighted, fertilising fields, and
all the time a store of salted carcasses
laid up in the cleitean to be shared. This was justice
indeed and crime unknown. Do you understand?
No such thing as crime. And nobody in thrall
to another man or woman, for the landlord
was like a god and absent for ever,
sending his minion but once every year
to take rent in avian kind back across the hazardous sea.

One day there came a steamship with strange people
bringing knowledge of markets. A world opened up
beyond theirs. And they put messages in bottles,
then trawlermen carried the word and later still
radio waves travelled over the sea waves,
and they were lost. They came within the compass
of the calculating world with its corpus
of laws and its religious integument.
They began to see themselves through others' eyes,
their children lulled with tales of another and better life.

Ill winds blew from all directions and they learned
what they could about saviours and sinfulness,
though their ways were ingrained and unreceptive
to crime. But the ropes that held them together
lay ravelled too long and their ankles grew thin.
At last they became a pure anomaly,
a just perceptible blot on the books
of the integral world. Their island was left
to the birds and what they left behind was lost,
to be stored in the cleitean of the afterworld's mind and preserved.

cleitean: small dry-stone, turf-roofed structures

BAGGAGE

I could have told her about the different parts
I played to suit the time and place, my bold flirtations
with danger, my hidden possibilities, my talent
for profundities after the event, the hearts
I could have broken if only I'd landed the first blow,
the serviceable nature of my conscience, the road
paved with good intentions that I started out on
from a childhood misted over like the window
of a closed-up house, how I've had it in the neck
since then, everything from love bites to the pain
of parenthood, the hopes and fears, the heavy stuff,
the baggage I lug around like Sisyphus's rock.
But I've always found it easy to leave things unsaid.
The body, though, has a language all of its own.
And mine was naked and unable to dissemble.
So I said nothing and let my body speak for me instead.

THE CHUTE OR NOTHING

I think of those who have no voice when people prattle
about being free to choose. Freedom's not what it seems.
I recall the factory that made fodder for cattle
where I humped sacks from a belt to a lorry with teams

of men who damned the government for burning a hole
in their pay-packets but soaked *me* with scorn for daring to say
they should join a union, which view a management mole
was quick to pass on to his keepers, who the next Monday

informed me that I'd been switched to what they called the chute,
where chemicals were dropped to coalesce with other goo
for the poor cows and where my sole companion was mute
except for a hacking cough given him in lieu

of a gold watch and where every time we tipped the bag
we released a swirling cloud of dust that stung my eyes,
filled my nostrils with a stench that caused my guts to sag
and lodged in every fibre and every pore for days,

so that my spirits sank to the lowest bovine plane
and at night I lay in a cold sweat, tied to a rack
on which slaughterhouse images hijacked my brain,
till on the Friday I meekly asked if I could go back

to the loading bay, anything but that, and was told
it was the chute or nothing. — I had nothing to lose.
I was a student. Disinclined to have my life controlled.
I told them where to go. Freedom's not having to choose.

THE KNOYDART HILL-KEEPER LOOKS DOWN ON HUMANITY

I want no company in this fastness.
Sufficient to me are the bonny beasts
that hold their heads high in the cloud mist.

Long may this heart of the rough bounds
remain unpierced by roads.

Let not my view of the grey, bonding sea
be spoiled by one of those shifty creatures
peering back at me through field glasses, a politician
scared shitless by the sight of savages appraised from afar.

And may those below me let me be, the odd incomers
who have newly taken up residence
to witness the end of our old ways.

Dregs of the Saxon brewer washed up on the cleared shore!

Sheep-like legatees of the ironmaster's ruminant estate!

Their crafted dreams are not darkened
by what history wrought.

How little they know how many silencings
made possible the silence I now enjoy
between the lochs of heaven and hell

up here with the stags, seven hundred strong,
and the seven hundred hinds and calves
that I never tire of seeing.

I give thanks that I can keep these hills.
I pray that I and those I cherish, the deer,
will not succumb to the iron law,
to the businessman's relentless forgings.

Let me continue to stalk where shielings stood,
at the furthest remove from the low plans
they pursue in their boardrooms.

Let me stand upright in the fierce wind
of a world that is corrupt beyond reckoning,
that has placed my beloved beasts on balance sheets.

The *politician peering through field glasses* is a reference to events in
1948, when the "Seven Men of Knoydart" challenged the property
rights of their absentee landlord, Lord Brocket, who was intent on
reducing the crofters' holdings on his sporting estate. A Labour
Secretary of State came by ship to view Knoydart from Loch Nevis, but
did not go ashore.
The *Saxon brewer*: Lord Brocket.
The *ironmaster*: James Baird, a nineteenth-century "laird" of Knoydart
who put his sheep on the hills following mass evictions.

STITCHED UP

Life, could it be, I wondered aloud, that the boots had worn thin
with which you kicked me in the teeth again and again
and that your steel-tipped assaults had finally ended?
But I opened my mouth too soon: they were just being mended.

CHAMPION

He ruins their game. That's what they say.
Blows them off the court on seventy cigarettes a day.
He's the world champ in the seventy-plus category.
Smash? He once smashed an entire set of crockery
after losing. At forty-two he won a set
against a Wimbledon semi-finalist; lost a bet.
His closest call was just missing the firing squad
in a Japanese POW camp. Talk about the fear of God:
he came home smoking seventy a day.
He was twenty-three when he started to play.
How far might he have gone? He's not one to brag.
His chief regret is not being allowed a drag
between games. And why not? Suzanne Lenglen drank gin
between sets. He'd be even better, he says with a wicked grin.
He has a heart of catgut and the face of an elf.
He'll never lose again to anyone older than himself.
He scowls at them like Lendl, he says. Plays with an old Dunlop
    Maxply wooden frame.
Plays disguised drop shots. Ruins their game.

DIOGENES
(A POEM FOR AN UNCYNICAL AGE)

D. was born in the sticks in Asia Minor, and like the other sods
And clodhoppers he whored and gambled his youth away,
Till he was drawn to Athens, inevitably you might almost say,
In search of brighter lights, better openings. Against all odds
The downward spiral of dissolution was arrested
In a bar, by a chance encounter with a maverick don
Who was telling all and sundry religion was a con,
While philosophy's way was truth that could be tested
In the crucible of virtue, and sooner than choke in the fog
Diffused by the Academy, the smoke-rings of cerebration
Smothering wisdom in never-ending speculation,
It would be better by far to lead the life of a dog.

Cynical, indeed. For this, D. discovered, was Antisthenes,
Who didn't give a Greek fig for the usages of society,
Taught in a gym, rejected Plato and his stuffy piety
And had studied under the hippest sage of all, old Socrates,
Who'd proclaimed that the king among men was he who was wise.
D. quizzed A. about his shabby gear. It was hardly like a king's.
Go naked, man, said the eccentric A. Cast off clothes and rings,
All that confines. Virtue's the cover you need, all else despise!
D. felt excitement in parts he never knew he had — his brain.
He decided to stop wasting time, wise up, get the lowdown
On that old master who'd drunk hemlock, wear a scruffy student
   gown
And enrol as a Cynic. In a word, he was born again.

He practised self-sufficiency: simple food, coarse apparel,
Slept rough under ancient porticoes in the shopping mall
Till at last, clinching his status as a cult man and oddball,
He found the perfect rain-proof bed in an ancient barrel.
In summer's stringent heat when others lolled in shade, he'd roll

In blistering sand, and in winter embrace the snow-cold stone
Of statues. Such was the way the dog-like Cynic strived to hone
His mind to the moral perfection that was his highest goal.
That his mood was nearly always tetchy, his manners rude,
Is a point in his disfavour. If it's not fun, then where's the sense,
After all, in becoming wise? Let us note in D.'s defence
the rigour of his life, the folly of the multitude.

Human meanness snares us all, be we sociable or otherwise,
Fate lays traps for philosophers and unsuspecting fools.
D., a stickler in his scorn for worthless social rules,
Fell among men who knew none: pirates who saw him as a prize
Like any other, not a detector of lies and counterfeit
And no, not an unchainable watchdog of morality
— you can imagine how, at that, they would have laughed
    uncynically —
and who without compunction sold him into slavery in Crete.
This unexpected metamorphosis from citizen
To helot left him somewhat underwhelmed: asked what trade he
    plied
By curious Cretan folk who knew no better, D. replied:
I'm what can best be described as a governor of men.

That a person can be bought and sold, a mere commodity,
Is thoroughly uncivilised. The ancient world, in this respect,
Crudely violates our modern sense of what's correct.
And since Cynic's no longer written with a capital C,
D.'s fate may seem to us ironic. This is a matter for debate.
What's not is that the pedagogical occupation
Is best performed by one for whom it's truly a vocation,
Like a Cynic. The gent from Corinth who now controlled his
    fate
Reasoned thus and freed the very man he'd lately bought,
Appointing D. as tutor to his offspring for the usual fees.
Historians tell us this monied man was called Xeniades.
One would like to know his views on the way his kids were
    taught.

Even those who do not seek it and never deviate
From duty's path may yet find fame, and this is consolation.
The mighty Alexander announced after due consideration
That if he couldn't be D., then he was glad to be Alex the Great.
The meeting of these luminaries was less than satisfactory.
It should have been, *avant la lettre,* a mediagenic spectacle.
In the event it proved to be short and undelectable.
Alexander was naive, D., as usual, was refractory.
I'm A. the Great — I'm D. the Cynic. These, suitably short,
Were the intros. The potentate then asked, quite properly,
In what way he could oblige the master of philosophy.
You can step out of my sunlight was the philosopher's retort.

Our conscience, like flesh, is weak and all praise is therefore due
To the unlikely lone campaigners who, upright and proud
And weather-beaten, through thick and thin remain unbowed
And, like a weathervane that's stuck, point only towards virtue.
So D. be praised. He died in Corinth in 323 B.C.
And even though — he wasn't one to carry papers — no-one
    knows
His date of birth, they say he was ninety when he turned up his
    toes,
Which shows it can't be all that bad to lead a life of austerity.
He left no lengthy treatises for posterity to scan.
He walked the talk, not only said, but also did what's right.
He was the unsurpassable Cynic who in broad daylight
Could be seen on the streets with lighted lamp, looking for an
    honest man.

SLAUGHTER-AND-BURN, 2001

Mediaeval man was unenlightened. The beast!
The weak were butchered and heretics were flayed.
Smoke filled the darkening sky from west to east.
It's no wonder there wasn't a tourist trade.

He made some truly memorable speeches.
Who remembers them?
He had a way with words.
Yes, he had his way with them.
He was the voice of the people.
Confused, contradictory.
He had real charisma.
What happened to it?
He had a vision for the future.
Memoirs are a nice little earner.
He had all kinds of great ideas.
And we couldn't be bothered to listen?
He was going to get things done,
   he was going to change the face of politics,
      he was going to revolutionise the way we live.
Him and whose army?

IN THE TIME OF THE GREAT MIGRATIONS

To reach the promised continent,
To sleep on a street in southern Spain,
With cardboard as your firmament,
You will cross the Sahara alone
On foot. You will flee from the light
Of all Africa. You will play dead
On the sea in a narrow boat,
Take any chance with men and God
To be given a chance to share
The world's impartial wages.
To stand in line at the kitchen door
Of the house where the party rages.

GOOD RIDDANCE (1999)

How you said GOOD RIDDANCE to the eighties, Hugh,
On New Year's Eve of eighty-nine, and how

It struck me as odd is what now comes to mind.
Odd to look at time, whose passing we tend

To regret, in that way. But you were saying
A silent valediction to something

Broken, I believed, while outwardly bubbling
With hope for the future, fired up and babbling

Like a prophet of a new dispensation,
The New Year's Janus face of negation

And affirmation. Our slates were wiped clean
In the year's first cold light. Brush and pan

Got rid of breakages, while the dynamics
Of social change would sweep Reaganomics

Into the same rubbish bin of history
As the fallen dictators. All so easy.

Easy to say. A marriage on the rocks,
That was hard. You'd had your share of bad breaks,

But disdained to look back, as now I do too.
This year of ninety-nine's fit only to throw

Into the memory's recycle bin.
And I'm not talking about the millennium

And all that madness, but the mutilation
Of life and language, the coronation

Of madness, madness to the nth degree
Of laser precision. You know the country

I'm talking about, for I know you once had
A friend from Belgrade. Didn't she go mad,

Long ago, long before that communiqué,
That apotheosis of perversity

With its sick, rehearsed alliteration,
Confirmed our century's degradation?

A country that didn't exist any more,
Fated for something that resembled a war.

And if it was in our own back yard, that war,
So what? Nothing can surprise us any more,

Hugh, ten years on. It was just one among many
At the dead end of our compliant century.

What can we say of them, if not GOOD RIDDANCE?
There's nothing else between screaming and silence.

Nothing can strike us as odd, nothing amazes,
As this year ends and the century closes.

UNIMPEACHABLE

The discordance of public discourse pains.
We know too well the rogues' fine suits and furs
hide stark naked untruth. But we're bound by chains
of office *they* wear. A vague protest stirs

inside us. We realise that the non-sense
loosed on the land is the language of the pricks.
But console ourselves that however dense
its structure, we can dismantle the bricks

to reveal a bedrock of mendacity.
We miss the point. The distinction between fact
and fiction is no more. Their capacity
for self-serving is nothing but an act,

consummately performed. This art's protection
from all probings. We ask what's hers, what's his.
Is it possible to make a connection?
They answer: *It depends what you mean by "is"*.

GONE WEST

First night in *Paradiso*. Foreign body.
Displaced. But freedom of movement
is assured on the way to the bar.

And then across a new floor
eyes trade their very first glances.
Body takes a position on a high seat,

divested to the thin veins of an obsolete
dignity. Unbodied words
— they say *I am Ukrajins'ki* —

spiral like smoke-rings. Nobody
understands. Body presents itself
in a foreign light. As hostess.

Hands take turns to hold a cigarette.
To hide behind, body has nothing else.
Language is broken.

EACHDRAIDH A' GHEAMA
(*HISTORY OF THE GAME*)

In an age of darkness lit only by sword and fire, the Norsemen —
they of the long ball — came in their long ships and proceeded
to spill blood and swap pennants with the hardy Gaels and
thereafter marked out playing fields throughout the Hebrides and
Man. These preliminaries, unlikely though it may seem, ushered
in the golden age in which the game flourished under the benign
sponsorship of the Lords of the Isles. The first match, which was
broadcast in song by the bards, was between Benbecula and Skye.
In fact, the Wingèd Isle can be said to have led the way, for
among the league's founder members were Kylerhea Rovers, the
renowned Borreraig Celtic and Minginish Thistle. In due course
the game reached unrivalled heights of artistry, its international
standing was on a par with Ireland's and it is reputed that crowd
trouble was unknown.

But at length the lowland kings, those covert devotees of the
English game, promoted in insidious fashion rival associations
and clan-based team selection. This led perforce to fierce and, it
must be granted, sanguinary encounters. In short, the English
style of kick-and-rush prevailed. Purists decided it was time to
make a stand, and duly challenged the Sassenach foe to a two-leg
affair. Amidst hurried preparations a French coach with
something of a reputation was hired. But, alas, his tactical switch
from all-out attack to timid defence went right against his team's
best instincts. And the English, perfidious as ever, fielded strikers
of every mercenary hue. The result: a debacle! Bitter divisions
among the supporters confirmed what had long been suspected:
the glory days were no more.

Proud but chastened teuchters were now reduced to turning out
for so-called British selects on foreign fields. And foreign to their
nature was the regimented game. All they won was decent kit
and the concession that their beloved pipes might be played

before the action began. The pay was poor. Back home, the supporters were hassled without mercy by the police and were even banned from wearing their distinctive and colourful gear, while the homely stadiums were turned into sheep-pens. Over the years they were cast in all airts, ending up in far, desolate places with unglamorous leagues. Today their descendants carry with them memories of a past they never knew, idealised it's true, though one that has substance nonetheless and sustains them in their humdrum lives like a plaintive song, like a battle-cry.

CONFERENCE CIRCUIT

The air is rarefied. Journalists are sniffing around
like tracker dogs. The conference centre is trying hard
to produce a buzz of excitement, but most of the noise
is coming from the whir of cameras and the croaking
of media frogs. The show is going out live. Power-
suited gurus are about to let their light shine
on major global issues. Masters of synergy
will open windows of joint opportunity. People-
sensitive strategists are going to empower
the man and woman in the street, while faith healers
of the market economy prepare to hawk rationalisation.
Agendas come out of hiding. The future waits
to be won. The latest lances are ready to be broken.
An expert in global troubleshooting projects himself
towards the mike. Flashlights are flashing. Cameras
are homing in. Media frogs can't stop croaking
and journalists are still sniffing around. The show
is going out live. A definite slight buzz can be heard.
Larvae are crawling back into the woodwork.

ICE AGE

For an age his only company is the icicles
that form each night on the mute ceiling
of his cell, and a black-bound book,
with its stories of miracles and forgiveness.
For an eternity this is everything.
This is his life, a mere incident
in the cold war. To have nothing,
all he has to do is deny it.

*Kim Sun-Myung was incarcerated for 43 years in South Korea for
communist sympathies, 35 of them in solitary confinement. He could
have been released earlier if he had renounced his views.* (The Observer,
26.1.1997)

LIBERATION DAY, EINDHOVEN

It's fifty years on and nobody wants to forget.

Like this old maid at the roadside
waiting for a local hero on a bike.

When he wanted to go out with her at sixteen,
father said wait another year, local hero or not.
What would the young man do when he stopped riding his bike?

She's waiting patiently enough. Though it's hard to believe
he'd come home on a bike from distant Neuengamme
after all these years. Even when they were courting
he wouldn't ride his bike in Germany, in Hitler's Germany.

Like the proud old tommies and yanks without warpaint
being borne along by jeeps.

Prizes to the south in Antwerp and prizes to the west
in Rotterdam, but never to the east. So many prizes
he drove a Studebaker, the only one in town. A car
fit for a wedding procession at eighteen. But father said wait
another year, Studebaker or not. What would they live on
later when the young man stopped riding his bike?

Like the peaceful liberators filing past
along Hell's Highway. Not one of them on a bike.
Not one of them wearing a striped jacket with a number on it.

Like this aged woman waiting with the patience of an angel,
hoping against all logic to discern a racing bike
among the armoured cars in the festive convoy
that's making its way to Arnhem fifty years on
(father said they'd have to wait for the end of the war),

waiting like one of those women I thought only existed in folk
    songs,
who stay true to their long-lost bicycle even unto the grave
(she might as well wait for Monty himself as her local hero),

watching the procession like an angel at a wedding,
among the crowd of people lining the road and greeting
the smiling veterans and conferring their benediction
and holding placards that say *Thank you for liberation.*

A POEM SHOULD BE LIKE A HENGE
      MONUMENT:
the words as well chosen
as the sandstone pillars and lintels,
hewn clean and set in perfect form,
bringing together, as the blocks were hauled up
by countless hands, the thoughts of many men and women
and so ensuring that something of them will survive,
and giving instruction and enchantment
and cause to reflect on their true meaning,
yet simple enough for children to play with,
as they might dance among the towering stones.

WHAT WE WANT IN ART

In art we want, as well as truth, an inkling of otherness, a sense
of longing for a better world. Whereas in life we fall short,
hard as we try. We may care that corporate America's wealth
derives from those such as the Indian left to die like rotting fruit
in Neruda's poem *The United Fruit Co.* But our anger
dies too. The composer Theodorakis must have known this,
for in his musical setting of the poem he chooses to render
the death of this *nameless thing*, this *fallen cipher*, incongruous
though it may seem, as a joyous climax of celebration.
In the poem it is cruel but truthful irony, and brings
to an end the portrayal of a continent's degradation.
The composer takes the poet's bitter words and gives them wings.
In his music-poem death becomes its own antithesis.
The Indian's dying is transformed into a triumph over death.
Thus, an all-transcending victory is won. And we get justice.
But only, of course, in the work of art. Where we want the truth.

CONFESSIONAL POEM

What if you confessed in a poem to having committed a crime?
I don't mean mere childish or youthful transgressions: you
    blamed
the demise of mum's best vase on your younger brother, you
    purloined
a 45 rpm from a charity jumble sale, you so
haughtily inflicted hurt on a diffident lover, and now
you must walk for ever bent with guilt. No, not that kind of
posturing, the beating of a puffed-up breast, the tossing-off
of a mea culpa, a cry released from the conspicuous heart.
No, I'm talking about full-blooded felony, the real thing.
You robbed the mail train in order to finance a revolution!
You did someone in, up a dark alley, for denigrating
your dear old dad! You committed lese-majesty
under cover of sunglasses and deadly umbrella!
And a policeman raps on your door. The sound is measured,
impartial, a fateful sound. His face is fashioned from granite,
it proclaims: I am incorruptible, I am interested
only in the literal truth, unadulterated. He is
of the species for whom poetry is suspect ipso facto
— though not in the habit of using the language of Ovid
and Virgil, he has otherwise mastered the turgid
but unequivocal diction of the servant of the law.
Thus he proceeds to ask you whether you are the author
of a certain published document, to wit etc, etc.
You admit it with a sneaking sense of pride, for as yet
you're unaware of the seriousness of your situation.
Yes, you say, yes, but of course it's only a poem.
The granite glints and wants to know if what you wrote is true.
True? Indeed it is, but this truth is, how shall I put it,
imaginative. The granite, lacking all imagination,
only hardens at this affront to literalness.

All he can imagine, you're sure, is your dog's bed
of an attic, with its cladding of coffee stains, paper
and underwear on the floor. The point is, you resume, it's art,
and art employs techniques of estrangement, the adoption
of a persona, a certain hyperbole, poetic licence.
The uniformed rock asks you to show him this poetic licence.
No, you stammer, there seems to be a misunderstanding,
you don't actually have a licence. But I have a warrant,
he says. And he thinks you'd better come along with him.
But this is insane, you say, no poet has done anything worse
than commit plagiarism. But then you think of Raleigh
in the Tower, Pound in a prison compound, and suddenly
you're afraid. Look, you say, I merely used some little tricks
— too late you realise that this choice of word is injudicious —
little tricks of alliteration, assonance, rhyme. And the crime
I confessed to was ... a metaphor, a symbol, a trope,
I'm not sure which. A tiny fissure appears in the rock,
the merest suggestion of a hint of a smile: Not sure, eh?
What I'm trying to say, you protest, is that poetry can't be taken
at face value; I wasn't writing about myself as such,
my concern was universal, the truth is we're *all* guilty.
Ah, that's interesting, he says (betraying no interest at all),
but I'm afraid, he says (abandoning literalness!),
that, be that as it may, you're going to have to come with me
down to the station, where you will be formally charged.
Formally charged! Oh, the sense of déjà entendu!
The expression means something totally different to you.
You can think only of your precious poetry, when
you really ought to be thinking about a lawyer.
You remember your posture, straighten your back and rehearse
in your mind a significant gesture, a clinching argument.
Look, you tell him, the truth doesn't actually matter —
people don't want the truth, they want to be entertained.
Really? he says, without raising an eyebrow. Is that so?
Of course, you reply, that's the real truth, I'm a poet, trust me.
Well, he says, I'm not and I don't. We go to the station.

OTHER TONGUE

It is my mother's tongue,
multiforked.
Before she was born
it had insinuated itself
like a serpent's
in black water
in a place it called Fermoy.

From my father I learned
how rich it is.
How it outspoke other tongues
from Kiltarlity
to Wounded Knee.

I was well schooled in it:
Here's the carrot of becoming
an anglospeechified top dog,
here's the stick to beat the boy
from the Scots-Irish bog.

I speak it in neutral tones,
unnaturally.
I shall always be tongue-tied.
I have only this other tongue
that cannot be unlearned.

I have only this language
imposed on me like a birthmark.
Its strange sounds brand me,
its blameless words.

SHARING

Imagine not being able to share
Those little confidences, whispered words
A bride shapes into a kiss. Imagine this:

Someone incapable of small talk, white lies.
Someone who magnifies. Imagine words
That never flower and yet grow so big
They can't be shared. Imagine a seedbed
Of blighted words, imagine waiting for them
To form long chains, hanging on them till it hurts.

For these are the words to which you're wedded.
And the only ones you truly share, truly
Tender words, are: Don't forget your medicine,
Your little drops, my love, in the ocean
Of our divided lives. My singular bride.

And the words that come to mind are: joy shared
Is joy doubled, sorrow shared is sorrow halved.
Words written in an album with pressed flowers.
Like a wedding vow. And that's what's hardest
To imagine: all you share is half-shared now.

STUDENT OF THE GAME

What a dipstick that Gazza thick as two short planks his
brains are all in his feet and look at the pesetas he's
earnin in Italy they don't know they're born these young
players nowadays it were different when I was a lad when I
used to watch City course most of em were part-timers
then remember Norman old Norman a big gormless lad a
cobbler by trade but he wouldn't stick to his last he
thought he was a footballer a centre forward they didn't
call em strikers in them days don't you remember him a
big awkward lad all elbows and knees about as elegant as a
pit prop didn't exactly look the part and to top it all he
was prematurely bald everyone called him a veteran before he
was even thirty God didn't he take some stick from the
wags on the terraces to be fair though he was good for the
occasional goal with his shiny old bonce but he wouldn't
stick to what he could do best used to put his foot on the
ball as if he was a continental you know tryin to do all
kinds of fancy tricks didn't go down too well with the
ignorant buggers on the terraces what did he think it
was first division I used to feel sorry for him when they
shouted abuse at him it was cruel it was poor old Norman
huffin and puffin he couldn't help it if he looked like a
geriatric eagle anyway why shouldn't the lad try that fancy
stuff come on Norman I thought score a goal and silence the
ignorant louts course they were just casual supporters you
know fair-weather fans they used to come traipsin over the
railway bridge a minute before the kick-off and jest their
way through the turnstile as the whistle blew and you could
bet they'd leave five minutes before the end of the match yes
off they'd go off home for their teas stone-cold certain they

knew the score and anyway if it changed they'd find out on TV that's not what you call a real supporter now I'll tell you what a real supporter is there was this old bloke I used to stand next to he'd be leanin against the crush barrier an hour before the kick-off brylcreemed hair a coat as thick as a rug reeked of woodbines a real student of the game he was evenin press in his pocket he really knew the game inside out even watched the reserves and he was like me he had a soft spot for Norman called him Twinkletoes gave the lad his due

THE BEAST WITH TWO BACKS

1

You throw tired old St Christopher away,
I'll put aside my digital watch
for ever or at least for a day.
Why this obsession with keeping time and making tracks?
Let's stay in one place and make the beast with two backs.

2

Forget the law of the market places —
We'll strike a deal with our improvident lips.
In that way we can show our true faces
and then trade with each other what the other lacks.
We'll make that unbusinesslike beast, the beast with two backs.

3

The name of the game is mutual attraction.
Only two people are needed to play.
It suits old hands like us to perfection:
We're rational human beings, not two crazy yaks.
So let's make that unbridled beast, the beast with two backs.

4

People have been told throughout the ages
to gather flowers before it's too late.
So follow the advice of poets and sages,
and forget all those horoscopes and almanacs.
We can make that fabulous beast, the beast with two backs.

5

We'll cast off the robes of hypocrisy
that are worn by timid, tight-arsed prudes.
We'll stand as naked as a new democracy,
put inhibitions behind us and get down to brass tacks.
We'll form a united front and make the beast with two backs.

KENNEN SIE HINCKLEY?

Every language has its lacunae. And yet
it seems those anthropologists who claimed
that the Inuits have four hundred words
for snow were greatly exaggerating
cultural diversity. Indeed, I clearly recall
a bierkeller in Hinckley. There's so much more
unites us than divides us. In indigenous tones
an entertainer, for lack of a better word
in our otherwise rich lexicon, a mardy sod
sang *Ein Prosit, ein Prosit der Gemütlichkeit*
and it was a dead end of summer Tuesday night
and anything but ger-moot-lish in that so-called
cellar. More like what the Scots call dreich.
And the fucking lager had lined my guts with ice.
But I thought I've heard everything now, I believe
in an underlying universal grammar, nation
can speak, *jawohl*, unto curious nation.

FIFTY-ODD QUESTIONS MY TEENAGE DAUGHTER DOESN'T ASK ME

why I was born
why my father and mother and their father and mother were born
who said So Be It

what kind of a piece of work I am
what expansive thoughts I harbour,
what hopes, fears, grand designs
of the imagination I entertain,
what petty real concerns bog me down

what's bugging me inside
what's tearing me apart
what's keeping my preposterous act together
why I assume this posture, why I pose
why I never suppose I might be an imposter
how I keep my composure

why I have this faraway look
why I'm like a closed book
why silence is my bottom line

why I'm a dreamer
and not a schemer
but have a mortgage, life assurance, a guard dog and a Beemer

why
    why
        why

why one thing always leads to another
        in our disordered world
            but something invariably fails to turn up

like that letter of recommendation posted to myself in my
    youth

what it was that made me think I was in possession of the truth

what it was like to be young at the dawn of the sixties
what I was doing when the president lied,
        when the wall went up,
        when the oily bubble finally burst,
        when the music died

whether experience can be bought for the price of a disc
whether wisdom raps in the street
whether enlightenment is worth the candle

whether we're not just horny goblins at the end of the day
whether our fissures and protuberances are all they're cracked up
    to be

whether it's wrong to love more than one
whether anything can be compared to love

        unless it be a perfect summer day
        or a songbird singing itself to death

whether selflessness is just another form of selfishness
and what's the name of the whole game if not hustling
        to get our genes into the next generation

into an indifferent future
        in which some greedy bastards will always grab the hog's
            share
        and science will no doubt find a way of getting a camel
        through the eye of a needle

how we can give purpose to our lives
        amid the utter purposelessness of nature
whether we don't need a project bigger than ourselves
        in order to be happy
what the old masters meant when they talked of reconciling
        honour and worldly goods and grace
and why I'm not quite cut out for happiness

what my aging heart thinks of the face in the mirror
what my eye doesn't see that my heart doesn't grieve
what I think in my heart of hearts
        when the show is over
        and I'm choked with emotion
        and knocked out by the products
        and the news has all been wrapped up for me

what I think of the role in which I've been cast
        in my little piece of the international action
what I think of the state of the world, of the nation, of the art
        of the possible or probable abuse of power
        at the beginning of the endtimes
        or of the countdown to a new beginning
and whether it makes any difference
        when I actually sit down and think about it
        whether I give it my best shot or the bras d'honneur

whether I feel truly at home in this web of interactivity,
        in the analogue body in which my heart is housed
whether I'm satisfied with the self-image I project,
        the way I refract and reflect,
        filter and select the light that others let shine on me

whether I'm at ease with myself,
>   untroubled by the psychic baggage
>   I bed down with each night,
>   the thoughts I lock out till the following day

and what earthly reason I have to keep looking forward
how I can have faith, when not a day passes without war,
>   in people or in some or in something or whatever
whether I know, at the end of the day, just what I'm living for
>   and what I should do before I shoot the crow,
>   hang my harp on the willows, turn up my toes
whether I don't know, in my heart of hearts, that the message
>   in a bottle will never be washed up on the shore
but whether I could ever doubt that we're right after all
>   to allow ourselves to be beguiled and regaled again and again
and then whether I'm well and truly sure, or whether I'm in two
>   minds

whether I'm really one person or two or three or four
whether I'm more than my name, my number, my status, my
>   title, my trade
whether the sum of my experience is greater than
>   all the stumbling walk-on parts I've ever played

*Those laws whose truth we learnt to the last letter
and thought we knew — with our last breath
we'll know we should have known better.*

TRAVELLERS

They feel at home, no doubt, in taxi cabs and planes
and to enlarge their self-importance speak
of the world as a global village. Let them walk
and prove their pins as feeble as their brains,

step after step as far as thin air will extend,
and look for her whose tracks I've lost for ever.
One small place would serve as well as any other
to prove to us the world is without end.

THE DEATHS OF HEROES

Though you can never be sure, I don't expect I'll have to stand
like Leviné before a firing squad, foretelling revolution
to the gaping barrels of the guns, or see my own defiant hand
severed from me, like Jara's, in summary retribution

in a deathly quiet stadium, or fall on distant arid earth
like Cornford, uncompromising against a world of heartlessness.
More likely I'll slump to a carpeted floor near my own hearth
or if I meet a violent death, then in a tangled mess

of metal on an unremarkable and familiar asphalt bed.
Death will don an ordinary black cap and will tie the noose
without any fuss. And dying will mirror the life I've led:
unheroic, private, full of passion that was seldom let loose,

caught up in the safety net reassuringly close to the ground,
far removed from the rarefied air of the higher regions
where the warrior saints and standard-bearers are to be found
and there's no place for the world's timid, leaden-footed legions.

— But with eyes wide open. If I wasn't cut out to follow those
who teach that all but a short life lived to the full is living a lie
and my own life is small in the shadow of the deaths of heroes,
still I know from their example: living is preparing to die.

7-6

The tie break is fast-food tennis. Must have been an American
 invention.
It saves time (it's money), lets the impatient crowd savour the
 tension.
You can win a set at a canter or by going through grief and
 heartache
after a six-all tie. It's worth the same. That's what's hard to take.
For instance, if you're Krajicek at the US Open playing Kafelnikov
and you lose two sets on tie breaks and what pisses you off
after you've won two with ease — 6-3, 6-1! — is that the tie
 break comes into play
for the final set too, for this is America, and you can't say
But I've won more points and games, I've served a record number of
 aces, damn it,
I've broken service five times to his one, let's slug it out, let's grand slam it,
not another tie break, please! Because rules are rules. And cruel.
The tie break is the moment of ironic truth in the dead-
 endedness of a duel.
At Wimbledon, against Stich, Edberg also lost three of them,
 won one "regular" set.
At the press conference he was a man looking for a hole in the net.
He'd finished up as loser with service unbroken. The serious
 Swede philosophised
about freakish fate. In his way the Swede was seriously
 traumatised.
With good reason. He would have to think all night about two
 shots he'd fluffed.
But at the end of the day he'd simply been Kafelnikuffed.
Or Stiched up, in his case. It happens to us all. Life finds out our
 flaws
and though we demand our portion of justice, life has inexorable
 laws.
Some seem to rise above them. Sampras has known almost
 nothing but glory.
Though once, at Wimbledon, he was Krajichecked. But that's a
 different fate, another story.

SOUNDS OF A VILLAGE

This ever so quiet village will be defined
for me always by the muffled shots that echo
over the gorse-filled moor from the rifle range
and by the silence of its departed players:
the doctor who left in the dead of the night,
going for abundance with the district nurse,
the former military man who decided
against misère and cut retirement short, leaving
a timid wife behind to stare at a photograph
of a son and listen to a gabbling daughter,
and then the constable and my grandmother,
dutiful, widowed, going solo for years,
who at last moved to the same dull plot of land
near the parish church to lie not too far apart.

Only a discarded old woman, shuffling
over the street and parroting daft refrains
from pop songs, remains from a childhood that seemed
never-ending, when I gazed from tabletop height
at those who were old but never grew older
as they gathered each week to play solo whist:
the debonair family doctor who smiled
so reassuringly and wondrously cured
my chicken pox, the retired army officer
with the handlebar moustache who lived in Briar
Cottage with a little chutney-making wife
and gave me postage stamps from the Gold Coast
and Gibraltar, the strong-suited, red-faced bobby
and grandma herself in her buttoned-up dresses:

all of them indestructibly part of a place
where life seemed larger and louder than anywhere
I lived later, all of them belonging there
as I never belonged in any town I knew,
putting right the world from Strensall to Suez,
bantering and laughing and clinking glasses
together, and only admitting silence
to the table in the deadly seriousness
of the game, allowing me to look at their cards
but not speak. The one who was dealt the worst hand
endures even now. She never came to play,
she didn't belong. Shrill and stuttering, her voice
still pierces the wholesome air like gunfire
and puts trusted clocks into quiet confusion.

TEN REASONS WHY THE ENDING OF OUR RELATIONSHIP HAS BEEN GOOD FOR ME

1. I'm losing weight: I'm being whipped into shape by sorrow.

The other nine I'll think of tomorrow.

LEAR

That things might change or cease, he says, switch off
That bloody box. Enough thunder, enough blood.
Your eyes are cold. Too many games. And there's
No game, he says, that's not a zero-sum game.
Win-win is a big lie-lie. No pain, easy gain
For some. For the rest, into Blawearie wi' 'em,
The cold blasted heath over which no bridges
Will be built to the future. Can't you see, he says.
Soon it'll be an ice-box. Don't you hear the news,
He says. Man beats man, batters woman and child,
Baits dog. Who bats an eyelid? The old manic
Inhumanity. The war games. Poisoning
Of the very air. Pillage. Eyeless corpses
Left rotting on a dunghill. And the bloodless
Bulling and bearing too that makes millions
Starve. Switch it off, he says, stop watching, will you.
Does the truth not lie in irony, paradox,
And is it not so that you've no eye for either?
So stop watching and do. Your eyes are bloody.
Stop watching and look at the tattered rags
And brittle bones, stop selling them short, he says,
Don't be so bloody-minded. And if still you look
With a cold eye, he says, then for this coldness
And this hardness, for this purity, this pure
Bloody blindness, you'll be visited, 't would be
Justice, by another ice age, he says,
Pitiless

51

NO ANSWER

That poet, that poet who sat
on a stone, sat on a stone
with his legs crossed, that German
poet of the Middle Ages who just sat
there pondering, who sat
on a stone pondering
how to live, sat there seriously
pondering how best to live, how
to reconcile worldly possessions
with honour and something else
I can't recall, though it was a serious
question, a question of great social
and philosophical import, it was
something to do with chattels and honour,
something along those lines, and possibly
something like spiritual grace, which
meant a lot to people in those days, but
he didn't provide any answers, I remember
that, he just sat with his arm propping up
his chin, sat on a stone and asked
that really important question, but
he didn't give an answer

TO EACH HIS OWN

(Suggested by the novel What A Carve Up! *by Jonathon Coe)*

Let justice prevail at last
and our dying become the way we live:
those who deal in arms have their arms cut off,
those with respect for the life of neither man nor beast
be forced to watch their own lifeblood slowly ooze away,
those who deal in untruthfulness choke on the words they're
    made to eat,
and let the deserving go gently back from where they came,
let their death be a moving earthwards in a dream.

ADDENDUM

The Chilean poet Nicanor Parra
spoke wisely when he said that
anything goes in poetry
so long as you improve on the blank page.

Sounds easy?

Yes, but think of unmarked paper:
where are the false pretensions,
where are the lies?

OTHER BOOKS FROM SHOESTRING PRESS

MORRIS PAPERS: Poems Arnold Rattenbury. Includes 5 colour illustrations of Morris's wallpaper designs. "The intellectual quality is apparent in his quirky wit and the skilful craftsmanship with which, for example, he uses rhyme, always its master, never its servant." *Poetry Nation Review.*

ISBN 1 899549 03 X   £4.95

INSIDE OUTSIDE: NEW AND SELECTED POEMS Barry Cole. "A fine poet ... the real thing." *Stand.*

ISBN 1 899549 11 0   £6.95

COLLECTED POEMS Ian Fletcher. With Introduction by Peter Porter. Fletcher's work is that of "a virtuoso", as Porter remarks, a poet in love with "the voluptuousness of language" who is also a master technician.

ISBN 1 899549 22 6   £8.95

TESTIMONIES: NEW AND SELECTED POEMS Philip Callow. With Introduction by Stanley Middleton. A generous selection which brings together work from all periods of the career of this acclaimed novelist, poet and biographer.

STONELAND HARVEST: NEW AND SELECTED POEMS Dimitris Tsaloumas. This generous selection brings together poems from all periods of Tsaloumas's life and makes available for the first time to a UK readership the work of this major Greek-Australian poet.

ISBN 1 8995549 35 8   £8.00

ODES Andreas Kalvos. Translated into English by George Dandoulakis. The first English version of the work of a poet who is in some respects the equal of his contemporary, Greece's national poet, Solomos.

ISBN 1 899549 21 8   £9.95

LANDSCAPES FROM THE ORIGIN AND THE WANDERING OF YK Lydia Stephanou. Translated into English by Philip Ramp. This famous book-length poem by one of Greece's leading poets was first published in Greece in 1965. A second edition appeared in 1990.

ISBN 1 899549 20 X   £8.95

POEMS Manolis Anagnostakis. Translated into English by Philip Ramp. A wide-ranging selection from a poet who is generally regarded as one of Greece's most important living poets and who in 1985 won the Greek State Prize for Poetry.

ISBN 1 899549 19 6   £8.95

THE FREE BESIEGED AND OTHER POEMS Dionysios Solomos
In English versions. Edited by Peter Mackridge.

ISBN 1 899549 41 2   £8.00

SELECTED POEMS Tassos Denegris. Translated into English by Philip Ramp. A generous selection of the work of a Greek poet with an international reputation. Denegris's poetry has been translated into most major European languages and he has read across the world.

ISBN 1 899549 45 9 £6.95

THE FIRST DEATH Dimitris Lyacos. Translated into English by Shorsha Sullivan. With six masks by Friedrich Unegg. Praised by the Italian critic Bruno Rosada for "the casting of emotion into an analytical structure and its distillation into a means of communication", Lyacos's work has already made a significant impact across Europe, where it has been performed in a number of major cities.

ISBN 1 899549 42 0 £6.95

A COLD SPELL Angela Leighton. "Outstanding among the excellent", Anne Stevenson, *Other Poetry*.

ISBN 1 899549 40 4 £6.95

BEYOND THE BITTER WIND: Poems 1982–2000, Christopher Southgate.

ISBN 1 899549 47 1 £8.00

SEVERN BRIDGE: NEW & SELECTED POEMS, Barbara Hardy.

ISBN 1 899549 54 4 £7.50

WISING UP, DRESSING DOWN: POEMS, Edward Mackinnon.

ISBN 1 899549 66 8 £6.95

CRAEFT: POEMS FROM THE ANGLO-SAXON Translated and with Introduction and notes by Graham Holderness. Poetry Book Society Recommendation.

ISBN 1 899549 67 6 £7.50

PASSAGE FROM HOME: A MEMOIR Philip Callow. Angela Carter described Callow's writing as possessing "a clean lift as if the words had not been used before, never without its own nervous energy."

ISBN 1 899549 65 X £6.95

Shoestring Press also publish Philip Callow's novel, BLACK RAINBOW.

ISBN 1 899549 33 1 £6.99

For full catalogue write to:
Shoestring Press
19 Devonshire Avenue
Beeston, Nottingham, NG9 1BS UK
or visit us on www.shoestringpress.co.uk